Dear Dara
and Robin ~
You are Earth Angels
spreading light, beauty,
and goodness in a world so
much in need!

Loving you always ~
Rebecca & Bill
July 2017

THE
ANGEL
BOOK

❖

A Handbook for
Aspiring Angels

❖

BY KAREN GOLDMAN

Illustrations by Anthony D'Agostino

❖

SIMON & SCHUSTER
New York • London • Toronto • Sydney • Tokyo • Singapore

SIMON & SCHUSTER
Simon & Schuster Building
Rockefeller Center
1230 Avenue of the Americas
New York, New York 10020

Designed by Charles Kreloff
Manufactured in the United States of America

9   10

Library of Congress Cataloging-in-Publication Data is available.

ISBN: 0-671-79699-2

DEDICATION

*T*o my beloved father, Morris J. Goldman, M.D., my first and very dearest angel, who taught me everything there is to know about angels, and showed me the reality of Heaven on Earth in the short time we had together before he went there himself. . . . To Kirk Wilson, my beautiful, dear friend who helped me to believe in angels and was called to Heaven too. . . . To my grandmother "Nanny," Esther Hassuk, my cherished kindred spirit. . . . To "Aunt" Debbie Tuchinksy, one of the kindest angels of my life, who taught me the generosity of a caring soul and the beauty of a loving heart (and to "Uncle" Arthur, the angel behind her). . . . To Thomas Campbell, my closest fellow angel, who nudges me upward when I waver and never lets me fall too far. . . . To The Sedona Institute, where I learned the Sedona Method® RELEASE® Technique, the use of which was instrumental in the writing of this book. . . . To Self Realization Fellowship. . . . To Simon and Garfunkel, who inspired my first thoughts about angels for this book at their incredible concert in Central Park, New York City, 1981. . . . To the part of every living creature which is an angel. . . .

ACKNOWLEDGMENTS

Many angels have helped this book come into being. I'd like to thank my agent, Al Lowman, for his amazing intuition and masterful business sense, and because he's a profoundly sweet guy. . . . Friends Jackie and Brian Peters, who appeared at just the perfect moment in my life with selfless determination and love to help this book get off the ground by getting my feet on the ground. . . . My acting teachers Silvanna Gallardo and Billy Drago for their brilliance, faith, and friendship, for always encouraging and reminding me to be myself, that I'm enough and that it's O.K. to be different. . . . My dear angelfriend Annie Helm, whose suggestions and love push me so gently to progress in all the right ways and literally helped the book get out into the marketplace. . . . My editor Patty Leasure for her intelligence and artistic sense, and her kindness and patience in our hurry. . . . Tony D'Agostino for his wonderful, inspired, and magical art. . . . And Marianne Williamson for her enthusiasm about the book, and her generous assistance in connecting *The Angel Book* with major-league publishing angels, thereby getting this project the first-class treatment it has received.

Contents

Foreword

Welcome to *The Angel Book,* a gift from angels everywhere to every heart. *The Angel Book* is the first handbook ever for the aspiring angels within us all, designed to help us understand and experience the essence of angels.

It is a description of our journey back to our own "lightest selves," not some farflung celestial creatures with harps and feathers. It is a book about all of us, just as we are inside right now, a road map to the higher realms within us. A love letter from our angels, our Heavenly counterparts, it is, therefore, a handbook to Heaven.

For the first time, angels are revealed in a contemporary, insightful and personal fashion which richly satisfies our wishful yearnings for proof of their existence and of their love for us. Most importantly, we finally discover for ourselves what being an angel is all about.

The Angel Book captures the essence of angels; we learn what it means to fly, how to make miracles, and get our own wings. We also discover what will happen when we become angels right here on earth—the privileges and soul joys, the ecstasies and rewards all angels experience, whether human or Divine.

The Angel Book will show us where to find our nearest angels so that we can ask anything we want to know, all by ourselves, anywhere, anytime, and for any reason.

At a time when the world needs angels more than ever, *The Angel Book* brings Heaven down to earth and lets us in on a precious discovery, a private and beautiful world—the inner world of angels.

For both seekers and sophisticates, people of all ages, backgrounds and cultures, it is the perfect year round gift to oneself or a friend. *The Angel Book* helps us to recognize and acknowledge who we are at our very best, and sends an honest message of love and encouragement that will linger.

A book whose time has come.

As you read and reflect upon your own life, allow your soul to dance across these pages as perhaps it has never really danced before. . . .

Simply be the angel that you are. Think beautiful thoughts. The angels will be listening. . . .

INTRODUCTION

——

The Mysterious Question of Angels

——

*I*f this were a book about a very rare species of tropical birds, or flying saucers, the Loch Ness Monster, or even something as ethereal as rainbows, clouds or stars, it would not be impossible to furnish a photo of one. We've all heard of people who claim they've seen goblins, gnomes, elves, fairies, beings from other planets, ghosts and even saints performing miracles. But just think for a minute. When have you ever heard of anyone who has seen an angel?

❖

People who have seen angels are rare, and those who speak of them are few. The stories written about angels are almost always fictional. There are many people who claim a sense of Divine intervention in their lives, and many more who admit feeling the presence of angels guarding and protecting them. But for most people angels are still hidden in the

shadows of religion, floating above us somewhere, quite invisibly. They are like secret friends watching over us, but rarely intervening. We hardly ever think of them unless we're faced with catastrophe or doom. Still, for those who do believe in angels (and our numbers are many), whether we remember them very often or not, just the thought of their presence, the very notion of them, is somehow comforting and adds a sweetness to our lives as nothing else ever could.

❖

Angels have been spoken of by all the greatest saints and prophets and poets throughout history. They've been sung about and dreamed of, sculpted and painted, and hung from windows and ceilings through the centuries. Angels are mentioned hundreds of times in the Bible. They have always been included in our most intimate prayers and sought out for comfort and advice at critical times. We cannot overlook them as a part of our existence. We don't really want to neglect them as a part of our experience. But where are they?

❖

Maybe we have been looking in the wrong places. Maybe they have been right here before our very eyes, somehow, all the time. Maybe we have simply been too busy to see.

❖

There is an unmistakable and profound reason why every culture, every religion, every nation down through the ages and in every part of the world extols angels as fit representations of man's highest conception of love and goodwill. They affect our highest senses, inspire our noblest thoughts, reflect our greatest aspirations. It is because at the core of our humanity we are really all very much alike on this earth, not in our animal-ness and mortality alone, but in our spirit. When we get to the level where angels do exist, there's really no difference between any of us.

❖

Angels have always seemed as elusive as the wind—as hard to capture as happiness itself, or love. This is because the important part of angels is not physical. Like happiness and love, they are also unlimited, eternal presences.

❖

Our questions about angels will always arise whenever we try to view them from a distance. But like love, if we look inside ourselves to understand the essence of just one "angel," we'll find that we can easily understand all angels.

❖

On that note, let's begin the angel notes. Read carefully and ponder well, because the things that are said here about angels may one day be said about you . . .

16

PART ONE

—

FINDING
ANGELS

—

I

Where Are Angels?

Wherever there is love, there is an angel nearby.

The pathways of angels are marked by beautiful moments, tender gestures, sweet gifts to the soul. To find all your angels, just remember, the mark of an angel is love.

❖

Angels are everywhere. They manifest their love through every heart, every honest smile, every act of kindness, every constructive thought. Their signature is in everything that grows, every selfless desire, every playful pirouette of every soul.

❖

Angels are always trying to reach you through your good thoughts, your inspirations, your warm feelings. Through music, art, drama, the written word. Also through flowers and sunshine and rain. There is always an angel somewhere trying to communicate with you.

❖

The presence of angels can be felt in every atom of creation. They are a part of the sweet feeling—the music behind all things visible which the pure of heart can hear and see.

❖

❖ Angels come in all shapes and sizes and colors.

❖ Angels occupy the loveliest corners of our thoughts.

❖ Heaven is the most natural place for an angel to live. (Naturally, wherever an angel lives feels like Heaven.)

❖ Angels always know where to find you—even when you're hiding.

❖ Angels don't disappear—even if you pretend they don't exist.

● Angels don't fall out of the sky; they emerge from within.

❖ Angels often work behind the scenes.

❖ In the darkest regions of the earth, the universe, and our being, there are always angels watching.

❖ Angels are speaking to everyone. Some of us are only listening better.

❖ Angels often go unnoticed. This is no discouragement to an angel.

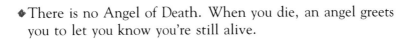

◆ There is no Angel of Death. When you die, an angel greets you to let you know you're still alive.

❖ Angels are never too distant to hear you.

❖ Angels never travel far from Home.

❖ Angels in olden times were just like angels now, except maybe a bit more dramatic.

❖ You do not have to go somewhere to be an angel.

❖ Whenever you feel like you're in heaven, you are.

II

How to Find
Your Angels

It takes an angel to know an angel.

*I*f we could perceive our angels for just a single day, this world would never be the same again, nor would it ever wish to be.

❖

We must not think angels have been hiding from us simply because we haven't known where or how to look for them. Angels have always been our friends. They are not only in books, on Christmas trees and cathedral walls; they are among us every day of our lives. They are not only on the periphery of our lives; they are with us now, if we would only recognize them.

◆ If you seek an angel with an open heart, you shall always find one.

❖ The only way to know an angel is by your feeling.

❖ Sometimes you only recognize an angel by the wings you find that you yourself have grown, just by knowing him.

❖ Angels may not always come when you call them, but when you need them.

❖ One reason no one talks much about angels is that angels are pretty quiet about themselves.

❖ Keeping an eye peeled for angels is never disappointing.

❖ An angel may become known to you through simple acts of kindness.

❖ Sometimes you know an angel only by the miracles he leaves blossoming in his path after he is gone.

- There is a kinship among angels everywhere that can never be erased nor broken, no matter what the trials and distances that seem to part us.

- On earth, an angel's wings are inside.

III

What Is an Angel?

Angels are reminders of what we're really here for.

Angels may be likened to great poetry. They lift the soul out of its cage of limitations. They return the heart to a reflection of its larger, freer self. They bemuse the spirit with at least a sparkle of the raptures of Heaven. And when an angel reminds us, for even an instant, of our own journey Home, our place of Origin, our lightest Self, it has caused a miracle within us. And that is not only the greatest poetry ever known to the soul—it is *Everything*.

❖

If we ever wish to know angels for what they truly are, perhaps it is we who first must learn to fly.

- An angel is a whole being.

- An angel is not a thing. An angel is someone . . . like you.

- An angel's song is sweeter than any bird's, any river's, any sound known on earth. Their music is not based on sound. They are the instruments of love.

- The sound of an angel's voice can unlock your hidden feelings.

- Angels sail through our lives like ships of light visiting us through the portals of our hearts.

- Angels reveal the presence of goodness in all things.

- Angels make us feel welcome in this world.

- Angels give us direction.

- Angels bring out the goodness in us that is ours already.

❖

WHY THEY ARE HERE

Angels are here to show us our own possibilities. They are here to let us know we haven't been forgotten. They are here to extend a hand to us whether we need a lift or not. They are here to re-acquaint us with everything wonderful about living. They are here as a gift.

IV

Who Are Our Nearest Angels?

Angels are the bright lights in the midst of our lives.

There are those who are very special to each of us—maybe not throughout our lives, maybe not for very long, maybe only in passing. But they make up the most beloved and cherished group we each have. These are our nearest angels, and as things turn out, often we are theirs too.

❖

Even if most of us haven't been blessed with visions, visitations or even dreams of holy angels, we mustn't think for a moment they have forgotten about us or gone away. It is our seeking that will first reveal angelic presences in others, and within ourselves. Then, one day, when we have really learned to fly in our own lives, we will find legions of these heavenly friends at our side so that together we can help others.

❖

We've never had to look far to find our angels. Angels have never really been out of reach. We can always discover angels from the inside-out, because it is the angel inside us who can point the way to all our other angels.

❖

Angels have more meaning than just as characters in stories from the distant past. In fact, they are members of a cast who make appearances in our lives every single day.

❖

❖ An angel is someone who helps you believe in miracles again.

❖ An angel is someone who brings out the angel in you.

❖ The sweet souls who love, cherish, inspire and protect the angel in you are your guardian angels.

❖ Everyone has their own angels.

❖ An angel is someone you're always very happy to bump into.

❖ An angel is someone who raises your spirits.

❖ A stranger who looks you in the eye with love is an angel.

❖ An angel is someone you feel like you've known forever even though you've just met.

❖ Anyone who helps you to grow is an angel.

❖ Everyone on earth will be an angel for at least a moment.

❖ There are often people nearby who want to pull you up when you reach out. These are your angels-in-waiting.

❖ It doesn't really matter how long angels stay in our lives. What matters is that we love them. Because through our own love, they can teach us all about Heaven.

❖ Angels are always memorable because they never forget what really matters.

❖ An angel appears to be just like everyone else, only more so.

❖ Angels are the entertainers who make the world laugh again when it's been weeping, and make us remember who we are when we've forgotten.

❖ Anyone can be an angel . . . to you.

❖ Sometimes even your worst enemies turn out to be angels after all.

❖ Whenever you are loving someone you are being an angel.

❖ An angel is you without any bindings.

❖ We're all angels in training.

❖ You don't have to die to become an angel.

PART TWO

—

THE
ESSENCE OF
ANGELS

—

V

What Does It Feel Like to Be an Angel?— Flying

An angel is like an arrow of light cutting through the dark.

The pure joy angels feel is like fresh air for the soul. Like a skylight opening, the angel within you can illuminate any circumstance and see everything in a perfect natural light once more. The angel within us is our most basic soul, unfettered. It is our simplest self when the pretenses and labels are cast away and our spirit is left to its own enjoyments. In this simplicity we are most profound. We are clean, clear, open, able, not needing to prove ourselves nor outshine anyone. An

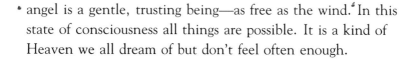

angel is a gentle, trusting being—as free as the wind. In this state of consciousness all things are possible. It is a kind of Heaven we all dream of but don't feel often enough.

❖

"Flying" is natural to an angel. We don't have to move through air and space to fly. This freedom and privilege has always been ours.

❖

Living in this state of love even for a little of the time can help those around us and, in fact, the entire world.

❖

❖ An angel is like an open window.

❖ Being an angel is like being in love.

❖ There are no strangers to an angel.

❖ To angels all roads lead to Heaven.

❖ Angels are really very down to earth.

❖ Angels have nothing up their sleeves.

❖ Angels reveal the beauty in all things.

❖ Angels never give up, they just let go.

❖ An angel's flexibility comes from humility.

❖ There is always enough angel to go around.

38

- An angel's voice is beautiful because he always speaks the truth.

- Anything seen through the eyes of an angel can be holy.

- An angel can always be profound, but doesn't have to be.

- There are no strings attached to angels.

- Angels don't like to be put up on pedestals—what elevates an angel is high thinking.

- Angels may not always be pretty to look at but they are always beautiful.

- Angels travel light.

- The world may push and pull, but an angel keeps his sense of balance.

- Angels walk softly and carry a big presence.

- An angel's intelligence is not merely of the mind, but of the whole soul.

- To angels, miracles are miracles no matter how ordinary they are.

- Angels stand on their own two feet.

- An angel's spirit is the spirit of friendship.

- An angel's intuition makes life seem like a dream.

- It is always thrilling to be an angel, even for just a moment.

- Angels appreciate the kindness of others.

❖ Angels are infinitely stronger than they look.

❖ When an angel talks, people listen.

❧ An angel's art is his heart.

FLYING

The angel within us is our private bridge to Heaven—the bridge that spans the distance from our average, mundane existence to the most heavenly thoughts, feelings and experiences; from our deepest misery to our utmost joy, and then, to the angel in others. To an angel, this joy has no boundaries, no name, no object. It is pure and eternal.

❖

There is really only one path to Heaven. On earth, we call it love. The moment we choose, we can let go and lift ourselves up to our very own angelic nature to find Heaven. This blissful state can never really be lost nor forgotten. If we feel it even fleetingly for a rare moment now and then, capturing it forever and becoming one with it eventually becomes our cherished, private, inner purpose.

❖

❖ An angel's love is weightless.

❖ Angels are light because they carry no burden of pride.

❖ An angel, like a butterfly, knows it is a great privilege to fly, even if only for a moment.

❖ Angels are not afraid of love. Love is what lifts an angel.

- Angels are willing to fall on their faces once in a while for the privilege of flying.

- Angels move with a heavenly gait.

- There is no challenge or paradox in life too steep for an angel. . . . This is where wings come in.

- Angels may have risen above a lot of things but there is nothing beneath an angel.

- Angels naturally gravitate upward in life. To angels things are always looking up.

- An angel's wingspan is broad enough to lift the heart of the entire world.

- The current beneath an angel's wings are feelings of love and happiness.

- People do fly. . . . Angels walk the earth. . . .

VI

How Do Angels Make You Feel?– Opening Yourself Up to Angels

An angel doesn't have to be physical to touch you.

Angels give the world something unique and special in life—something intangible that stays with us for the rest of our days. We can never forget them, nor what they give us. Nor can we ever repay them, except by giving the same thing to others. That's the way angels work.

❖

Angels help us gather our forces and let down our walls. They show us the safety and freedom we inherently have when we

are in tune with our higher angelic nature, and how we can never make a false step when we decide to love.

❖

Always be aware of the presence of angels in your life. When you trust and tune in to angels you will be divinely protected and guided in life in the most heavenly ways.

❖

- When you are lost in life, an angel will get right inside your heart with you and show you the way home.
- Just being around an angel can make you feel free.
- Angels resurrect your faith in human nature.
- An angel's heart has room for you when you have nowhere else to go.
- Angels bring light into all your darkest places.
- Angels remind you that you are enough.
- Angels help you expand your heart further than you ever thought it could go without breaking.
- Angels shelter you with their presence but never block the light of day.
- Angels help you find your wings no matter where or when you think you may have lost them.
- Angels push you out of your little self and into the broad arena of love.

❖ The reason you love angels is because it is the angel inside you that does your loving.

❖ Give an angel an inch and you gain a ticket to Heaven.

❖ Angels always notice you—when you need to be noticed.

❖ Angels give you those gentle pats on the back you need to keep going.

❖ An angel gives you your very heart's desire sometimes as easily as though it were only an afterthought.

❖ The sound of an angel's voice can unlock your hidden feelings.

❖ Angels encourage your best qualities and hidden talents.

❖ Angels help you see your life in a better light.

❖ Angels appreciate things about you that you thought no one else ever even noticed.

❖ Angels help you find the courage to do whatever you were meant to do.

❖ Angels help you stay afloat with their unsinkable, buoyant natures.

❖ Angels help you laugh at life even when you don't think it's funny.

❖ Angels restore your will to love.

VII

How Angels Feel About You— Receiving Angel Guidance

Angels don't worry about you, they believe in you.

Angels care about us because they live close to their souls. It takes great courage for us sometimes to show each other how much we care, but angels are never ashamed to let us see. They know it is not enough just to excel in life or merely to set a good example. As much as angels love their own freedom, they want us all to know how to fly, too. The closer angels are to Heaven, the more they want you to discover your own wings. An angel could never feel "lonely at the top." In their hearts, they take everyone with them.

To an angel, your company, your friendship, is a privilege. You are always welcome in Heaven.

❖

While as mortals we struggle to find our place in life, angels know that in our essence we are all really in the same place, and will never take advantage of our openness.

❖

• Angels never bother about the mood you may be in, your past, or whether you consider yourself "spiritual" or not. They see you for what you really are—an angel. And, no matter what, to an angel that is always holy.

❖

Angels can work with us only to whatever degree we are able to hear them. When we are willing to grow, they will lead us. They are only waiting for us to pause . . . and ask the way . . . and listen. Such are the ways of angels.

❖

Whenever we need love, we need only to be open ourselves because angels are truly everywhere—kind beings who only want to help and to love us.

If we are not receiving what we need, perhaps we are not quite as receptive as we think. When Divine company arrives, we must let it in. Angels will never impose upon us nor disturb our privacy. If they find the door to our hearts closed, they will not enter.

❖

For every willing soul, there is a willing angel.

Angels aren't seeking your love, they're only loving you.

No matter how much trouble you may have believing in angels, they still believe in you.

Angels reward your love with an expansion of your own being.

Angels don't blow their own horns. They find it makes living much too noisy.

Angels never want anything from you except your own happiness.

Angels don't want to impress you, just to bless you.

An angel knows just what it feels like to be you.

Angels often see you accomplishing your goals before you can see it yourself.

Angels stand by you even in the darkest hours of your life.

Sometimes angels treat you as though you were the most wonderful person in the world.

❖

The qualities that seem heavenly in people and all creatures really are conceived in Heaven. Each time we perceive the beauty in another person, the same chord of feeling is touched in us. The same melody begins to play. In love, there is a great music between beings. Whenever we feel we are seeing someone's soul unmasked, that's the angel in us seeing the angel in them. It's as close as we can be to one another. It is a sacred moment in time. We know we are the same. We know then what it feels like to be angels.

❖

❖ An angel respects whatever is really important to you.

❖ Your success will make an angel happy.

❖ Angels always think you're worth the effort.

❖ Angels trust that we each have our own runway and will take off on schedule.

❖ Angels respect your right to be Human.

❖ Angels are most inspired by your wish to be free.

❖ Angels are never too shy to tell you they love you.

❖ An angel will never leave you . . . in spirit.

❖ Angels would rather give you their love than keep it for themselves.

❖ To an angel, forgiving is just another form of giving.

❖ Angels see right through your walls.

❖ Angels do things you thought no one would ever love you enough to do.

❖ To angels you are special, because you are you.

VIII

What Do Angels Do?– Heaven on Earth

Angels light the way.

What is considered "genius" by the world is simply the "angel" within us acting without our interference. This is how great men and women function. It is how great, brilliant and masterful works are done and how man's "greater purpose" can be realized. Those who enter this dynamic and powerful state uncover the heavenly realm of angels.

❖

Throughout history our most accomplished artists, musicians, writers, actors, scientists, architects, engineers, athletes, dancers, philosophers, philanthropists, religious figures and world leaders—all earth's heroes—have been men and women

who crossed their own bridges to the angel inside themselves.
They allowed the angel within them to excel and to fly. Often
their primary purpose was simply to help others. This loving
intention is so powerful it can lift us out of our own sense of
limitation and allow us to achieve real greatness.

❖

To be truly wise and powerful on this earth, we must only
allow ourselves to be, and to express freely, the angels that
indeed, we already are inside. Our noble and exalted works
will follow along with our highest achievements and our
rewards. We are all essentially capable of greatness, of genius,
of soaring beyond the mundane. While as human beings we

are filled with limitations, the "angel" inside us knows none. It is unlimited and eternal. Everyone is gifted. The "angel" within us is our gift.

❖

You can never fail when you are in line with the angel in you. Everything you think, do and feel has limitless power from that place. How high and how far you may reach depends on your commitment to it. Within that commitment, your God-given freedom and the generosity of your own spirit are all the seeds of your highest glory.

❖

Abraham Lincoln, John F. Kennedy, Martin Luther King, Mahatma Gandhi . . . your brother, your dentist . . . the lawyer . . . Picasso, Van Gogh, Mozart, Bach, Beethoven . . . Thomas Edison, Louis Pasteur . . . Mother Teresa . . . the grocer, the guy at the corner news stand . . . Shakespeare, Einstein, Plato, the lady in the next car who smiled at you, the Vet . . . Charlie Chaplin, James Dean, Judy Garland, Spencer Tracy, Shirley Temple . . . Jimmy Stewart . . . your Aunt Rose . . . the baby-sitter you had when you were nine years old, the little girl you saw yesterday at the bus stop . . . Michelangelo, Leonardo da Vinci . . . the Beatles . . . saints of all religions . . . the mailman, your first-grade teacher . . . Simon and Garfunkel. . . .

❖

Sometimes angels leave this world early so that we can feel what they mean to us and think about what they stand for and stood for in life.

♠

Angels can unleash hurricanes of healing, release tidal waves of love, move whole mountains of hatred, melt icebergs of jealousy, and evaporate oceans of pain.

❖

❖Angels rarely wait around for thanks.

❖Angels can do anything they set their minds to, because their hearts are set already.

❖An angel does not give up or give in. He just gives.

❖Angels walk the tightrope of life with amazing grace.

❖Angels are the best leaders because they follow their own intuition.

❖Angels don't always follow normal rules. They sometimes demonstrate better ones.

❖Angels always rise to the occasion.

❖An angel can do no wrong because his heart is in the right place.

♠Angels encourage everyone in the direction they really want to go . . . up.

* Angels don't worship their own acts. They act in a spirit of worship.
* Letting go is simple to an angel. That's what angels do best and is what gets a person off the ground.

❖

Study the lives of the great human "angels" who have lived. See what made them tick—what their priorities were—what they cared about.

❖

Angels are often bearers of good tidings, secrets, special information. They sometimes act as messengers of love between people. Angels today can use telephones, radio, T.V., books, movies, the mail and computer communications to deliver their messages.

❖

* An angel always cares when no one else wants to bother.
* Angels don't feed our egos. They nourish our being.
* An angel may save your day, and sometimes your whole life.
* An angel's hidden agenda is love.
* Angels keep going long after everyone else has given up.
* The warmth of an angel's light can comfort and illuminate the whole world.

❖Angels soften the roughest edges.

❖Even the slightest gesture of love can be grand when performed by an angel.

◆An angel does not run away from life, he flies toward it.

❖An angel doesn't hide in other people's shadows.

❖Angels do what they love just for the Heaven of it.

◆Angels plant seeds in people's heads—that bloom.

❖Angels always fly directly to the heart of the matter.

❖Angels accomplish the "impossible."

◆Angels don't do without, they do within.

❖An angel doesn't set limits for himself—he lets them all go.

◆If we were all a little more like angels, earth would be a little more like Heaven. . . .

IX

Children as Angels—
The Keepers
of Heaven

No matter what their size, angels are big in spirit.

•Angels are not physical, so they never grow old. No matter how many years you may live, the angel inside you will forever be ageless and youthful like a Divine and playful child.

❖

There is still a child in each of us that has always believed in miracles. To children, miracles are simple things. In childhood every day is miraculous—unexplained, inspiring, ever new.

❖

When we were small, we all listened to the angel inside us. It

was our loudest inner voice—all-positive, reassuring, comforting, encouraging. It was the voice of Truth beckoning us always on to our loftiest, most loving selves.

❖

When we rediscover angels in our grown-up lives we'll realize there is yet great hope for us. It hasn't really been so long; we haven't really grown old at all.

❖

❖Cleanliness may be next to godliness, but angels do come with dirty faces.

❖Children always believe in angels. It's mutual.

❖Whenever an angel wins, everyone feels like a winner.

❖An angel's beauty makes everyone feel beautiful.

❖Parents of small children can learn a great deal about angels simply by observing.

♦The light in children's eyes is the reflection of Heaven peeking through.

♦A child's laughter is much like the sound of an angel singing.

♦To an angel, everything is absorbed in joy.

❖You can always see angels' protecting light shining on the still faces of sleeping children.

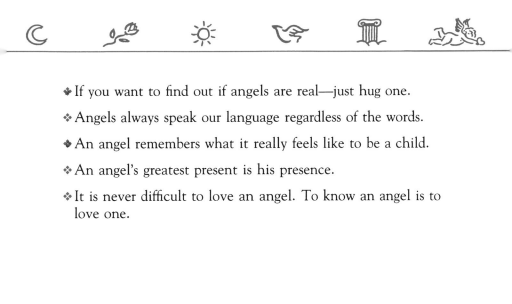

* If you want to find out if angels are real—just hug one.

* Angels always speak our language regardless of the words.

* An angel remembers what it really feels like to be a child.

* An angel's greatest present is his presence.

* It is never difficult to love an angel. To know an angel is to love one.

PART THREE

—

BECOMING
AN ANGEL

—

X

Rediscovering Our Own Innocence– Heaven

Angels hide nothing and therefore see everything.

•When we begin to rediscover angels in our "grown-up lives," we can begin to live once again without the weights of negativity, resentment, fear and hate that we have tied to our own souls. We will not lose our safety, clarity or stature by letting these burdens go—we will win back our lost freedom, our hearts and our wings. We will not lose our foothold, we will gain instead the grandeur of Heaven. ↵

❖

Angels are not naive simply because they are innocent. In an angel's innocence lies his brilliance.

❖

The difference between people and angels is only in our point of view. The path of an angel is basically the same as the path of an ordinary person—it's just a different altitude.

❖

When we feel and act as angels and do their work, what difference is there between us? Only in our thinking is there a gap. In our essence, there is none.

❖

You don't have to try to be somebody new or better or different to become an angel. Just recognize that you already are somebody perfect and heavenly. Then, just be you.

◆

As you become an angel you will no longer wonder whether your life has a meaning nor whether it has somehow passed you by. We do not have to acquire anything new to become angels—only to shift our point of view. We can move back to the heavenly part of ourselves from whence we came.

◆

- Whatever an angel is seeking is seeking him. Whatever an angel has found has found him.

- The difference between a person and an angel is not really so big, but it is a shift in commitment.

- An angel's heart sees everything as it really is and accepts it with love.

- Sincerity is the delicate fabric an angel's wings are made of.

XI

Divine Privileges and Miracles

• To an angel the sky's the limit. •

Each one of us may look forward to experiencing certain
Divine privileges and bonuses as we become greater angels.
An angel's rewards grow, deepen and expand to perfection.
There are countless benefits along the way. This is how saints
and prophets are known to live their lives. The inner peace
and goodwill of an angel can become imperturbable. Nothing
can bother the happiness nor peace of mind of an angel in his
highest natural state. Angels come to wholly identify with
Heaven itself. They say it is a boundless and unimaginably
beautiful existence. •

❖

Even the laws of nature bend to serve the goodwill of angels.
To most people these occurrences are called miracles. To an
angel a miracle is simply the harmony of love. •

❖

The highest angels no longer struggle but seem to attract goodness itself. They are filled with it, and indeed, because they release all else, they become it.

❖

• Only an angel can fully understand the simplest and most precious things in life like silence, friendship and compassion.⁸ Complexity can then be seen as only a vain creation of man.

❖

It is within the utter simplicity of our most quiet inner feelings that we may all claim the greatest wisdom and spiritual knowledge, and also reap the Divine rewards reserved for, and known only by, angels.

❖

❖ When an angel discovers himself, the universe lights up.

❖ An angel is somehow provided for, is never surprised, and is always grateful.

❖ Angels notice their dreams coming true all the time.

❖ Angels see the light at the end of all tunnels.

✦ An angel knows where light comes from.

❖ An angel's love stops time.

✦ Angels' souls are washed with joy.

❖ To angels, things are always looking up.

◆ Angels always get the best because they are giving it.

❖ Nothing could ever be too good for an angel.

◐ Angels make universes sing.

◆ Angels see light shining right in the center of the darkness.

❖ An angel's reflection is perfection.

❖ An angel's soul fills all holes.

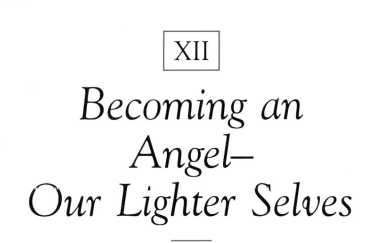

$$XII$$

Becoming an Angel– Our Lighter Selves

Sometimes all an angel really needs is a good running start to fly.

When you let your inner angel out to play, unusual forces come to your aid. Little miracles begin to happen all around you. Things take place for your benefit that seem to defy logic. Perfection begins to make itself known to you through ordinary events. You begin to unveil the deeper meaning of your life, the hidden truths of this world. You finally arrive at a profound and exquisite vision of the universe.

❖

There are no difficult rules or tests for aspiring angels apart from those that confront us through normal living, because all the answers to all the toughest questions are already inside you. An aspiring angel must never be afraid to ask the really important and interesting questions in life, because only in discovering where the answers lie will you uncover the angel in you and your nearest Heaven.

❖

There are as many ways of becoming an angel as there are angels themselves. There is no proper way to do it. It is not important how you become one. Any way you get to Heaven is just fine. Whenever the next moment arrives when you feel you are ready to fly, look around you. There are always openings in the field of angels.

❖

Your trip to Heaven is a journey only you can navigate for yourself. If you will listen to the angel inside you, you will find directions coming to you as sweetly as music.

❖

To become an angel you must discover your own inner light for yourself and let it shine.

❖To become an angel you must be willing to give your light to the world (no matter how it may be treating you lately).

❖A halo is the result of having one's head truly together.

- Becoming an angel is a lot like waking up in the morning. Everyone gets up when they're ready.

- Every time an angel transcends the gravity of life, his wings grow bigger.

- Becoming an angel never has to take time. Angels only live in the Now.

- The easiest way to find your angel is to simply notice it when it happens.

- The distance to Heaven is only as far as it is to your real Self.

- Sometimes it takes all your strength to be an angel. This is how you grow your wings.

- It is never too late to become an angel.

- There is a beautiful glow that comes over a person becoming an angel.

- Tears of joy are the mark of an aspiring angel. When the tears leave, you're in Heaven.

- To be an angel, love whomever you do love, completely.

- The nearer you live to your own angel heart, the nearer you live to Heaven.

- If you want to know where Heaven is, stop looking at your shoes.

- No one ever knocks an angel for trying.

❖Love is the only cushion that can stop a falling angel.

❖It's not even so terrible to be a fallen angel. Just get up.

❖

Angels may not be the complete answer to our everyday lives. . . . Then again, maybe they are.

XIII

It's Easy to Be an Angel– Our Bridge to Heaven

Being an angel is always simple. Not being an angel is what can get complex.

⸦ You will find your nearest angel not by identifying with your ego accomplishments, but by identifying with your soul accomplishments: the hurdles you conquer in life and the inner distances you traverse, to return always again to your own feelings of love and goodwill, your bridge to Heaven—your nearest angel. ⸧

❖

When we accept ourselves as angels, we are gifted, guided,

unified beings. Our natural mission is love. Our natural home is Heaven. God has given us this freedom. The reason we do not yet manifest it entirely is only our own silly selfishness, our pride and our ignorance.

❖

+ The fastest way to become an angel is to face that you are one already.

+ The more often you let yourself feel your own happiness, the more often you'll find Heaven.

❖ The intelligence it takes to be an angel is natural.

❖ To an angel, smiles are the next best things to halos.

❖ Angels often grow in spurts; you don't have to become an angel all at once. It's O.K. to ease into it.

❖ An angel's most precious possession is freedom.

+ To angels, laughter is the next best thing to flying.

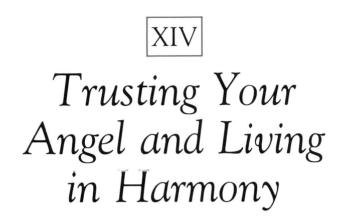

XIV

Trusting Your Angel and Living in Harmony

Shyness is only the angel inside us trying to get out.

The angel in you can heal you in many ways. Angels can help to heal illness, poverty, anger, despair. There is an abundance of pure healing energy, joy, creativity and unwavering inner strength available for you at all times. Protect these gifts. Dedicate your life to the splendor and oneness of purpose all angels radiate and share.

❖

When given permission, your angel will help you untangle seemingly impossible situations; support you through your worst fears; amaze you with brilliant thoughts and exquisite perceptions; bathe you in glorious feelings of ecstasy, joy, love, peace. This angel can reveal fascinating, sometimes lifesaving (or life-changing) things to you about yourself and others. Your angel can help you fight your battles, conquer all your inner demons.

❖

By surrendering to the wisdom and power of this angel, you will learn to keep your chin up through the very worst of times and let Heaven come to you. When the world gives you excellent reasons to give up, your angel will give you reasons to persist and be strong.

❖

When everything seems against you, stand by your angel. You will feel confident in a way that no one can take away knowing this intelligent, indefatigable, unwavering, glorious part of you is in control, deep within you, no matter what may happen.

❖

Pay attention to your own loving, lovely inner voice. It will keep telling you the truth; it will keep you from harm; look out for all your best interests and encourage all of your best advantages and opportunities. Right in the middle of a heated situation, stop. Be an angel and listen. You will be told how best to proceed. It's as simple as that. This angel will keep joy within your reach through the sad and painful times. Trust

your angel more and your limited "self" less. That is a piece of freedom.

Keep in mind . . . being an angel doesn't mean acting sweet and mushy all the time. 'Angels can be tough.'

◆Only your heart can lead you to Heaven! Even when someone else appears to be way out in front of you, your own angel is still your truest leader.

❖If you let the angel within guide you, you can never be misled.

❖Your own happiness is the best test of how you're doing as an angel.

❖Keep company with angels. Being an angel is contagious.

❖Only when we trust our own AngelSelves do we ever feel truly secure and at Home.

❖An angel doesn't care who's "on top." When you find your own wings it just doesn't seem to matter anymore.

❖No matter how tired of it all you may sometimes be, there is an angel inside you who is wide-awake and raring to go.

XV

The Wonderful Freedom of Living as an Angel

There is a freedom and harmony in the life of an angel that surpasses the imagination. It is beyond all the conceptions of the mind, like a beautiful breeze blowing through your life, massaging you, tickling your being, uncovering obstacles so you can go around them, opening doors for you, attracting all your heart's desires, pointing you ever toward the light. The angel within you possesses the keys to everything you ever wanted. It lives in eternal communion with the essence of all things. It is the doorway to your Home within, your inner haven of love, security, and peace. It is the guardian and keeper of your deepest, most personal remembrance of God. This angel is never meant to be hidden, but always revealed; not captured, but forever set free. •

❖

Whenever possible, cross the threshold of feeling to your own inner Heaven. It is your highest and most sacred right. No one can ever make you turn back once you do.

❖

TELLTALE SIGNS OF BECOMING AN ANGEL

As You Become an Angel . . .

. . . A lot of things that have always bothered you may not seem to matter so much anymore.

. . . Everything might suddenly begin making sense to you.

. . . Angels may begin to awaken all around you.

. . . Life may become a whole lot easier.

. . . You may find wonderful surprises coming to you out of the blue.

. . . Everything else about living may begin to feel extracurricular.

. . . You may find that you have become your very own shining light.

. . . You may find yourself doing something nice for other people.

. . . Your own world may begin to become like Paradise to you.

XVI

Accepting Your Angel and Getting Your Wings

Love is how you earn your wings.

° *R*ekindle your own perfect relationship with this most precious, innocent, powerful, graceful creature of light within you.˙When you feel one with the angel in you, you feel a oneness with Everything.

❖

By noticing your angel whenever you are happy, feeling loving, or feeling good, you can begin to identify it and learn to recognize what makes your angel come, what makes it go. You can make fully discovering your angel the object in your life. Then, one day, you'll identify with this angelic self alone and you will always be in Heaven. It is as actual as you are. It

is never separate from you. It is your heavenly soul—who you really are. It is you. There is nothing more that you could ever be.

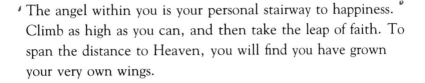

❖

The angel within you is your personal stairway to happiness. Climb as high as you can, and then take the leap of faith. To span the distance to Heaven, you will find you have grown your very own wings.

❖

The whole purpose of life is to know your AngelSelf, accept it and be it. In this way, we finally experience true oneness.

❖

Always realize how special this angelic part of you is—how powerful and how unique. Protect it, love it, nurture it in yourself and in others. Do whatever you must do to protect and free (and always appreciate) your angelic self.

❖

Accept it as natural for your angel to do well. The angel within you deserves the best and accepts it. You will find, as many have, that your wings were never really lost to begin with.

❖

❖ To an angel, to be truly human is to become Divine.

❖ It is your love that makes you fly.

❖ Your angel wings are made of love.

XVII

Working and Playing Together as Angels

There are magnificent angels doing things to help us right now in every part of the world. Be an angel. Join the club.

❖

Any effort no matter how small, even simply thinking like an angel, is tremendously powerful and could affect the world in a significant way. Certain powerful angels have been able to alter the entire course of history with one or two powerful thoughts. 'The simple vibrations of your loving feelings, your own angel thoughts, can affect others for the better. Send them out into the universe. Someone will feel it somewhere . . . an angel's love is never wasted. '

❖

Try the basic thought "I love you." This is the universal basis for all angel thoughts.

Your conscience is your angel talking. When you feel your heart open to ease the pain or share the joy of another, know that little crack in your armor is setting free the angel you have long kept shut inside you in darkness.

Do what will make this angel happy. Play. Don't worry about the results. Angels just trust. If there's one thing an angel knows, it's that support is everywhere.

Be an original. Angels are never copies, but always unique. Do things no one has ever done before. When you act as an angel, the way will be opened for you. Against all odds you will succeed.

There are angels all over the place just waiting to be friends, waiting to be awakened, waiting for a chance, an opening, to love you.

From this day on, wherever you go in life, try to see every other person's soul with your soul. See the angel hiding inside them. Embrace their hearts with your angel heart. The angel inside them will always rejoice, knowing it has found, at last, a true friend.

❖

Celebrate angels wherever you may find them, and you will find them everywhere. Cherish them. Give all your special angels many internal hugs. An angel never forgets to say thank you.

❖

Stand up for the rights of angels everywhere. The downtrodden need angels most of all. Let them know they're not alone. Keep reminding them in whatever ways you can that their own angels are still alive and well, living inside them. You will learn what even the mightiest angels know—that there has never really been a poor angel . . . because all angels are priceless.

❖

As you continue your angel work you will sometimes feel rushes of love coursing through you as though millions of angel wings were brushing through your entire body, your heart, your brain, every cell and nerve. This is the beginning

100

of ecstasy. If you listen closely, you will hear your angels cheering you silently on.

❖Only an angel can practice being one.

XVIII

Care and Nourishment of Your Angel

*L*et the angel inside you speak to all people and you will witness your life as a series of heavenly encounters . . . Be like a raindrop . . . Moisten the dry hearts of many people with your love, then watch them flower before you into beautiful angels . . . Honor all the angels you will now recognize in people everywhere . . . Greet every angel you meet with love . . . Always show your light . . . There is too much darkness in the world already . . . Take strangers into your heart as your own . . . See the angel in everyone and you will always be in Divine company . . . Don't be fooled looking for angels among only the wealthy, or the poor . . . Outward symbolism means nothing to angels . . . Theirs is a universal address . . . Respect all children as the Keepers of Heaven they are . . . They are aspiring angels too, and will help us as best they can . . .

Let your soul be nourished in its own light . . . Invite harmony and light into your life to find your Freedom . . . Live close to your soul ? . . Remember that angels are our very best examples in life . . . By nature we are like them . . . When we are not in touch with the angel inside us, we are simply not being ourselves . . . Everyone is an aspiring angel . . . Knowing it only makes the trip easier by our embracing it, and our surrendering to it.

❖

WHY THEY ARE HERE

Angels are here to prove that it is safe to trust each other, and ourselves. They are here to help us learn to determine our own destinies. They are here for us to better understand our own natures. They are here to invite into our most tender feelings. They are here as reasons for us to drop our defenses. They are here to open our eyes to our own wisdom. They are here to soften and end our self-hate. They are here to prod us into our own courageousness. They are here to patiently watch us fumble with a million things we should already know and encourage us to keep going.

The Angel Book is only a reminder. It is an arrow to Heaven. Use it for strength and stamina any time you feel you need an angel. The sentiments of all angels are reflected in these pages. Hold to these thoughts. Accept the loving feelings of your angels. They are on your side. They want your happiness. They want you to fly.

INVITATION FOR ALL ANGELS

Come fly with me beyond the stars,
   Beyond our fears, where angels are
And there together sit beside
   The hand of God.
We'll watch the day approach when we will fly.
   We'll see our many wishes touch the sky
And Happiness become a dream that
   Lives in peace and doesn't die.

ACTIVITIES AND SUGGESTIONS

Make a list of all your known angels. Keep adding to your list as new angels appear in your life.

❖

Highlight the sentences in this book that remind you of someone you know, and give it to them.

❖

Sponsor an angel. Put your picture inside the front cover of this book. Give it to someone you know.

❖

Write down all your own angelic qualities as they come to mind. Take some time to enjoy how it feels to be an angel.

❖

Think about the people you love. List their angelic qualities too. Think about how wonderful they are.

❖

Write about the most heavenly moments in your life so far, and what it was that made them so.

❖

List some things you have always wanted to do, that to you would be like flying. Decide you can do them. It's your birthright.

❖

Think about what you'd someday like to do for others.

❖

Ask yourself, if you had one gift to give the world, what do you wish it could be? Any angel will tell you . . . it is yours to give if you just give it.

ANGEL WISH

Whatever your path, your angels hope your journey will be sweet and that you sweeten the lives of others.

Advanced material and further heavenly secrets will follow, either in material form . . . or invisibly. . . .

❖

We will all be prophets when we tune in to Truth. We will all be masters when we can master our own unlimited possibilities. We will all be saints when we act selflessly, according to guidance from above. We can all be glorious, guardian angels right now, for each other, and of course, ourselves.

❖

Give yourself credit. You have the makings of a beautiful angel

❖

Trust the wings you have been given. You have earned them. You do know how to fly.

. . . CONGRATULATIONS . . . YOUR ASCENSION HAS BEGUN!

❖   ❖   ❖

*I*f you've had an angel experience—
feeling, vision, or encounter—
we'd like to hear about it.
Please send your story to:

KAREN GOLDMAN
8721 Santa Monica Blvd.
#118
West Hollywood, California 90069-4511